MY EIGHT GREATS

My Eight Greats

*a family history
in poetry & prose*

Lois Perch Villemaire

ELLENDALE PRESS

MY EIGHT GREATS ©2023
Lois Perch Villemaire
all rights reserved

ISBN 979–8–9887443–0–6

Ellendale Press

loisvillemaire@gmail.com

designed and produced by
Sarah Bennett

shbennettbookdesign.com

dedicated to
my mother, my father,
& my sister

Contents

My Family Tree

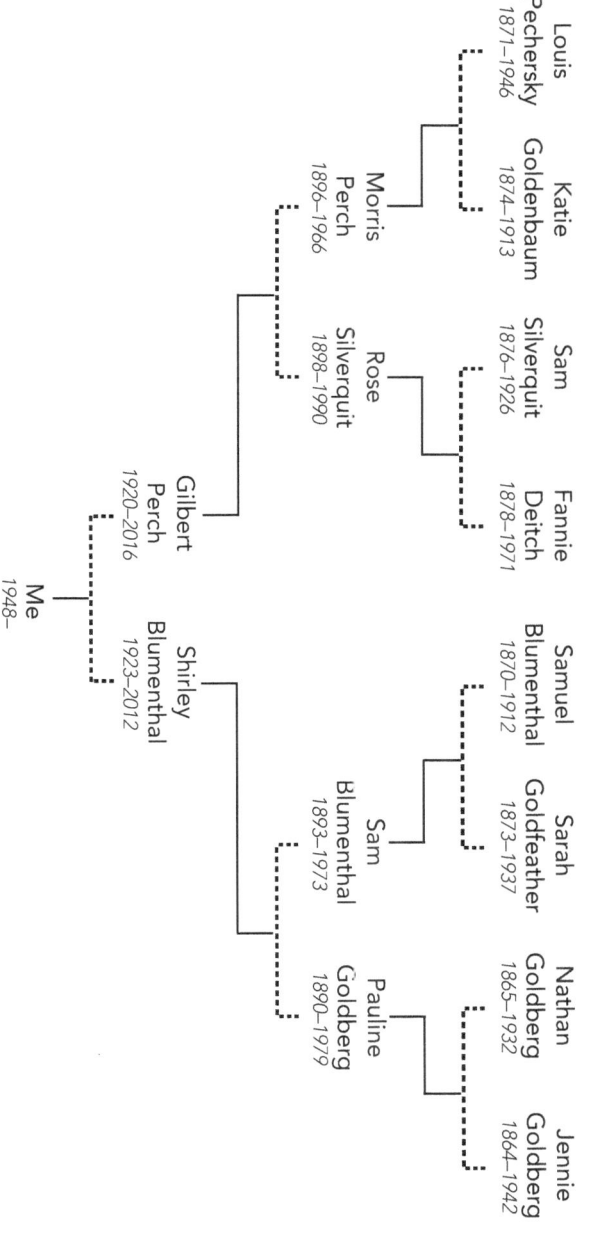

Preface

I became interested in details about my great-grandparents as I worked on building branches and adding leaves to my family tree on ancestry.com. I discovered they were born in small towns and villages in Eastern Europe between the years 1867 and 1878. I found old photos of their faces and felt my link to these eight souls—four married couples.

These brave men and women immigrated to the United States for safer and better opportunities by rail and then by ship, finally settling in the city of Philadelphia between 1885 and 1898. Some were meeting relatives or joining close friends who could provide security and guidance in the new land. The subsequent marriages of their children and grandchildren resulted in my birth in 1948. My DNA includes contributions from my "eight greats."

When I began to tell their stories in poetry and prose, they seemed to step out of the old sepia photos and emerge in bright colors. Although most of what appears in these pages is true, at times I have used my imagination.

Research led to learning more about my grandparents and parents. I was lucky to have close relationships with them during my childhood, teen years, and in some cases, well beyond. But what were they like as young people? What were their dreams? What lessons did they teach me?

Uncovering their stories is like trying to complete a jigsaw puzzle with missing pieces. It may be too late to find answers and sadly there is no one left to ask.

My wish is to honor them by passing along flashes of their lives, even if only through an anecdote, reflections and memories, or by sharing what I have learned of the challenges they faced. This book is meant to be a gift to my family.

LV

Acknowledgments

Grateful acknowledgments to the editors of the publications in which these poems and stories have appeared, some of them in slightly different form or with a modified title.

Blue Mountain Review: "When My Mother Got Her Drivers License" (2022)

Ekphrastic Review: "My Sister's Flair for Fashion" (2021); "When Memory Becomes Art" (2021)

Fewer Than 500: "I Remember Bobby" (2020)

Flora Fiction: "How My Sister Continues to Shine" (2021); "Isadore's Wallpaper" (2020); "To Jennie—My Grandmother's Mother" (2022); "Getting Through Winter" (2021)

Fresh Words: "Sentimental Reasons" (2022)

I Am My Father's Daughter: "My Father's Yiddish Letters" (2022)

In Her Space Journal: "On Not Choosing Paper Dolls" (2022)

Last Leaves: "My Grandmother's Dressing Table" (2022)

Moonstone 26th Poetry Ink Anthology: "My Mother Was a City Girl" (2023)

One Art: A Journal of Poetry: "My Father Collected Penguins" (2022); "My Mother Walked to John Story Jenks School" (2022)

Pen In Hand: "Closest To My Heart" (2021)

Potato Soup Journal: "Driving Lesson" (2020); "The Ball Collector" (2019)

Soul Poet Society: "7947 Heather Road" (2022); "What I Remember Is the Last Day of School" (2022)

The Drabble: "Wearing Her Jewelry" (2021); "What My Father Always Said" (2021)

The Post Grad Journal: "My Father Shines Like a Lighthouse" (2022)

The Ravens Perch: "My Mother Loved Dining *al fresco*" (2022); "Cameo Rose" (2021); "Discovering Those Precious Words" (2021); "My Father's Voice" (2023); "1112 Melrose Avenue" originally appeard as "Sea of Spindles" (2021); "Yesterday My Grandfather Was Buried at the Cemetery" (2022)

Trouvaille Review: "Best Mom" (2020); "Turning Myself Over to the Sea" (2021)

Truth Serum Press—Lifespan Series: "Bottom of My Heart" (2020); "Summers" (2021); "Flashes of My Grandmother" (2021); "How I Met My Second Husband" (2022)

100 Subtexts: "Ode to an Antique Music Box" (2022)

MY GREAT-GRANDPARENTS

If You Ask Where I'm From, #1
after George Ella Lyon

I'm from Poland, Lithuania, the Russian Empire,
small villages and towns,
Tulchin, Raseiniai, Kukla, Riga, Pruzana,
and the village of Shpikov.
I'm from a voyage across the Atlantic Ocean
on the SS *Buenos Ayrean* and other ships
to the docks at New York's Ellis Island
or Castle Gardens at the tip of Manhattan.
My eight great-grandparents would board trains
to join family members living
in the city of Philadelphia.

I'm from a shoemaker on Girard Avenue,
a family of seven living on the second floor,
a leather shop at 5th and South, bustling
with streetcars, carriages, and vendors.
I'm from the garment industry, a buttonhole maker,
a tailor, a carpenter who worked on
the construction and maintenance of Lucy the Elephant
located "down the shore" in Margate City, NJ—
the oldest roadside attraction in America.

I'm from families suffering losses of mothers
and fathers too soon to abandon children.
They had faith and community support
to lean on in onerous times.
I'm from traditional holidays,
food prepared by women who learned
from mothers and taught daughters,
hoped and prayed for safety and prosperity
for the next generation.

To Jennie: *My Grandmother's Mother*

I've known you only in three black and white photos
as a girl from Raseiniai in a pleated dress with ruffles
to the top of your neck sitting beside your sister
the hair on your forehead arranged in a perfect curl;
a mother circled by four daughters;
a widow in a shapeless black dress in 1942
nearing the end of life's journey.

You were the sorrowful bride of an arranged marriage
to an older man in another village in 1884
while your true love Nathan was directed by his parents
to make his way to America.
It was dangerous for young Jewish men
to be conscripted into the Russian Army.

How did it feel to have no voice or choice
when you were placed on divergent paths
never expected to cross again?
Nathan moved across Europe by train,
sailed on the *Polynesia* to Ellis Island.
Yet that is not how your story ends.

He sent for you and you arrived in Philadelphia,
holding the hand of your two-year-old son,
child of that arranged marriage.
How did you traverse 5,216 miles?
What obstacles did you encounter along the way?
In this new land you and Nathan created a family.
For me that is where your story begins.

Isadore's Wallpaper

ISADORE GAZED around his bedroom grinning at the zoo wallpaper. He delighted in the colorful cartoon animals that greeted him—pink giraffes, green lions, monkeys, and elephants. The wallpaper was pale yellow with light blue stripes, like cages at the zoo. When he wasn't feeling well and had to stay in bed, the animals kept him company. The seals balanced on balls, the monkeys hung from trees by their curly tails, while hungry giraffes nibbled at the leaves on the tippy top. Mother said he could go to the real zoo someday.

Isadore squinted as morning light filtered through the pink flowers on the dogwood tree that leaned against the house. He pictured himself climbing out the window onto the sturdy branches of the tree and making his way skillfully to the ground. Downstairs, he heard Mother preparing breakfast. The pop of the toaster and the whirl of the orange juicer made him hungry. The smell of coffee meant that he'd better rush to see Papa. As Isadore hurried down the steps he thought he heard Papa say "...this trip might be too much for him."

"Papa, do you mean me? We are going down the shore today, right?"

Papa glanced at Mother as his lips tightened into a serious face.

"Yes, but be careful. Enjoy Atlantic City. I wish I could go, but I have to work."

Papa picked him up for a goodbye hug, one that seemed to last longer than usual. He left for his job at the dress factory where Isadore sometimes visited. He liked running his fingers along the endless rows of hanging patterned fabric and watching Papa operate the noisy machine that made buttonholes. Someday he would teach Isadore to use the magical machine and they would work side by side at the factory.

Polly was included in the outing to help with her adored little brother. He had a Buster Brown haircut and the same clear blue eyes as the rest of the family but not the same good health. Dr. Gold made house calls to listen to his heart and check his breathing. Even though Isadore would soon be six years old, he had never experienced the excitement of Atlantic City.

They entered the busy Broad Street Station in downtown Philadelphia. Isadore was amazed to see so many people, especially other children like himself, on their way to an adventure. Inside the coolness of the train station, Polly buttoned up her brother's blue double-breasted coat. She and Mother wore long ruffled dresses with wide-brimmed hats. Isadore covered his ears when the steam of the locomotive pumped, and the powerful whistle blew. Isadore thought about the fun of being the train operator, the person in charge of that whistle. The platform trembled and it smelled like something was burning. Polly lifted him up to reach the steps into the train.

"May I sit next to the window?" said Isadore. He watched as scenery of a park flashed by and imagined the day that he would meet other boys and play baseball on a real field. After arriving in Atlantic City, they went by horse and carriage to an area with many hotels that had large, covered porches overlooking the beach. They followed the crowds to the bathhouses where a photograph souvenir was taken of the three of them seated in a special automobile. Afterwards, they rented bathing attire.

On the beach, Isadore liked the way the air smelled like salt and fish. There were colorful umbrellas and striped awnings arranged to provide cover from the sun. Isadore explored the gritty sand with his fingers and toes. He built castles and made footprints where it was wet and squishy. He thought about living in a house as big as a castle. He discovered slimy seaweed and collected seashells of all shapes. Isadore inched closer to the shoreline and Polly joined him as they held hands and jumped over small waves. He wanted to let go of her hands and dash off, diving into the biggest waves and swim all the way to where the pale green ocean met the sky.

Later, on the boardwalk, he was fascinated by the blinking lights, rows of rolling chairs filled with people, and amusement rides. He pretended to be a tough cowboy sitting in the saddle of a brightly painted wild horse on the musical carousel. He breathed in the aroma of roasted peanuts and buttery popcorn but didn't feel hungry. Isadore sat on a bench to rest a bit and began to dream about being in his bedroom. He imagined taking a magic carpet ride home.

When Isadore coughed so much that he felt too tired to walk, Mother and Polly took turns carrying him as they made their way back to the station for the return train ride. He didn't remember the bumps and sways of the train, Mother's soft humming, or being carried to bed. When he opened his eyes, he saw the zoo wallpaper and heard the familiar heavy footsteps of Dr. Gold coming up the stairway. Tears filled his eyes and his head throbbed. He practiced taking deep breaths and waited for the doctor.

Baba Flew in From Florida

I WAS SEVEN YEARS OLD. My great-grandmother was coming to visit. It would be my first time meeting her. She had moved to Florida when I was too young to remember. Dad told stories about how she would bake his favorite honey cake and bring him a piece at the schoolyard. He loved his grandmother and called her Baba.

It was the first time I'd been to an airport. The entire family was excited. Through a wall of glass, we watched as Baba walked down a long stairway attached to the plane. When she entered the terminal and came closer, I realized how small she was. Baba wore glasses and smiled, revealing tiny stained teeth. A fitted hat covered most of her brownish hair and earrings were pulling at her earlobes. We took turns hugging and kissing her. She approached me and cupped my chin in her smooth, cool hand before pulling me close. Her scent reminded me of our coat closet.

Everyone was amazed by how perky she appeared after the flight. She didn't even want to take a rest.

"She's fresh as a daisy!" said Dad. We took her home.

I was surprised by the way Baba talked. Her "w"s sounded like "v's". She spoke to Dad in another language. They must have been saying lots of funny things because they laughed so much. He told me they were speaking Yiddish.

During her visit, Dad used his new Polaroid camera, instantly developing my image with Baba, a photo I have cherished along with feeling grateful to have known my great-grandmother.

Now a grandmother myself, my childhood impressions of Baba were transformed when I researched the life story of this incredible woman. Fannie, as I have come to think of her seemed larger and stronger than the petite woman I first met.

She lived with her aunt in Poland after her parents died. At age thirteen she came to America to join her brother. Working as a tailor, he had saved enough money to fund Fannie's journey to Ellis Island by ship and then by train to Philadelphia.

Fannie found a job babysitting for the 3-year-old daughter of a man named Sam whose wife had passed away in childbirth. She soon became both the nanny and housekeeper. At the age of fifteen, Fannie married Sam.

Sam and Fannie had a daughter named Rose born in 1898. She had long blond hair and blue eyes. Fannie fixed her hair in braids. Sam loved to sing Italian opera and Rose took piano lessons. For a while he ran a leather shop on South Street but something at home wasn't right. Rose reflected many years later, writing about Sam on the back of an old photo, "… he stopped at every saloon and was quite tipsy."

In 1909, Fannie filed for divorce and became a single mother with an eleven-year-old daughter. Her stepdaughter had moved to live with relatives in New York City. I imagine that a divorce was unusual for a Jewish woman in those times. She must have been courageous and determined. Information during the next few years is vague, however Rose appeared in a formal photo with Fannie's brother's children, looking like part of his large family.

Louis, who lived in the neighborhood was left to raise two sons and two daughters after the death of his wife in April 1913. To continue supporting his family as a carpenter, he needed a housekeeper to cook meals and maintain the home. He hired Fannie.

The story of a romantic relationship between Fannie and Louis will forever be unknown. Did Louis fall in love with her and she with him? Was it a matter of convenience? Whatever the reason, their marriage took place in June 1914. They were married until his death in 1946. Fannie embraced the role of mother to Rose, stepmother, grandmother, and eventually great-grandmother to many, including her brother's children and grandchildren.

In 1968 at age nineteen, I flew with Rose to visit Fannie. Taking my hand, she showed me around her cozy space in an apartment hotel in Miami Beach. I was bewildered when Rose later said to me: "Baba told me to introduce you to her friends as her granddaughter. She doesn't want them to think she's old enough to have a great-granddaughter your age."

Perhaps she still felt young. That I can understand.

Years later when her health began to fail, Fannie/Baba, the family matriarch flew from Florida to Philadelphia to live her last months with Rose in a small apartment. She passed away at age 93.

(clockwise from upper left) My great-grandparents:
Nathan Goldberg, Louis Pechersky, Sam Silverquit,
Sarah Goldfeather, Samuel Blumenthal, Jennie Goldberg,
Katie Goldenbaum, Fannie Deitch

(above, l to r) Grandparents Morris and Rose Perch, great-grand-mother Fannie Perch, Shirley and Gilbert Perch c 1951

(facing page) Grandmother Rose Silverquit and great-grand-father Samuel Silverquit in Philadelphia, 1906

My great-grandmother Jennie Goldberg (l), her sister Bertha Goldberg in Raseiniai, Lithuania, 1883

My grandmother Pauline Goldberg (l) her mother
Jennie Goldberg, with Jennie's son Isadore Goldberg on their trip
to Atlantic City, 1912

My great-grandmother
Fannie Perch visiting from
Florida with my brothers
Gary (l), Brad, and me,
1954

MY GRANDPARENTS

My Grandmother, Cameo Rose

When my grandmother passed away
I acquired a piece of her jewelry
as a memento.
Nothing had been required,
she was unforgettable.

Never the type for fancy things,
a few familiar dresses, lipstick only.
Her love of family was sweet,
like the notes she played on the piano.

I don't recall seeing that cameo,
worn as a brooch or pendant,
framed by a lacy gold octagon border.
Delicate profile of a porcelain woman, hair flowing,
silver braided necklace with a diamond,
a rose in bloom carved on her shoulder.
Her name was Rose.

Was it a gift from my grandfather?
Or handed down by her mother?
Perhaps a favorite keepsake she'd had for years?
Touching and turning in my hands,
thumbs skimming the texture,
studying rise and fall of shape,
searching in vain for a hidden story.

My Grandmother Pauline's Dressing Table

As a child, I would climb onto the upholstered seat,
facing the mirror of my grandmother's dressing table
against the wall in her bedroom.

I would inspect each item as if it were new,
matching comb and brush, bottles of perfume, jewelry box
filled with necklaces, bracelets, and screw-on earrings.

Playing dress-up, I slipped on a bracelet or two,
dabbed toilet water on my neck imitating her
and running a comb through my curly hair.

I would reach for the silver-handled mirror
with an engraved design on the back to study my face,
brown eyes, freckles splashed across my nose.

Inhaling familiar scents, I would brush my finger
in the face powder, touch tubes of lipstick, eye color, rouge,
and fumble with the funny scissors
that curled her eyelashes.

A silver framed wedding photo taken in 1921
faced me on the corner of the table, my grandparents
watching me pretend I was grown up.

Flashes of My Grandmother Rose

My grandmother overflowed with love.
She wore her honey-colored hair in a bun.
As a child, I didn't realize it was a hair piece.
She loved holding babies.
My mouth dropped open
when I saw her bathing my newborn daughter
in the kitchen sink.

She loved to tell stories about family.
Why didn't I listen more carefully?
Or ask questions?
She held tight to your wrist as she spoke,
to convey the importance of what she was saying,
and so you couldn't walk away.

She loved to play the piano,
looking so natural on that bench, fingers dancing,
entertaining us with upbeat tunes
while she relished her role of providing
musical background at family gatherings.

She loved walking places,
turning down rides, even at 90 years old.
She loved to sew, donating sleepers
to the hospital for newborns.
She taught me to operate
her old black Singer sewing machine,
when my foot could reach the pedal.

Later, I came to understand
she had a difficult childhood.
Her parents divorced when she was 11 years old,
she lived with cousins for a while.

I came across a photo
of her posing with other female relatives
in 1919. Smiling young women wearing
men's hats and holding cigars
in celebration of the passage of the 19th Amendment.

Sadly, this incredible memory was discovered
too late for her to tell us the story.

Sam's Journey

SAM WAS a ladies' man. He was handsome and he knew it. He exercised to stay in shape and weighed himself everyday like a prize fighter. Before he left school due to family issues, he was on the track team at Central Manual Training School in downtown Philadelphia. He was a stylish dresser and took pleasure in wearing fashionable clothes.

Sam was neat and precise about his surroundings. He kept his section of the room he shared with his brother immaculate and posted a calendar where he carefully printed his scheduled appointments. Sam had excellent penmanship and enjoyed working with numbers. Arithmetic was his favorite subject. His parents told him that an education was important, so he paid attention in school.

Sam's father was also a good-looking man with dark curly hair parted on the side and a thick mustache. He and his young wife, Sarah immigrated to the United States in 1890, settling in Philadelphia near his older brother. They both worked as shoemakers.

There came a time when everyone thought Sam's father had become an alcoholic. He began to stagger when he walked and slur his words. Sam was embarrassed by the changes in his father but at the time, no one knew the real reason for his odd behavior.

People avoided him and his shoemaker business declined. Sadly, this caused a loss of contact with his extended family. In a matter of months he died when Sam was a teenager. An autopsy revealed it had been a brain tumor. The year was 1912.

After her husband's death, Sam's mother was left to raise five children. She continued his business by hiring a young shoemaker to run the store and compensated him with room, board, and a small salary. Sam and his two brothers had to find work to help support their mother and two young sisters.

Sam wasn't interested in the family business. He found an entry level job with the Pennsylvania Railroad but soon discovered that it wasn't for him. With his outgoing personality and easy smile, he found it boring to work as a laborer. He gravitated to selling produce and working in a local grocery store, discovering he loved pleasing customers. Sam set out to learn all he could about the food business and dreamed of opening his own market.

He worked long hours and on his days off, Sam looked forward to riding trolley lines to explore different sections of Philadelphia, a city with an established and expanding public transportation system. One summer day, Sam hopped on the Route "23" electric streetcar that stopped near his home. He planned to investigate an area in the northwest direction of the city. With the windows down, he was cooled by the breeze as the path of the steel tracks twisted and screeched through ethnic neighborhoods. As Sam heard foreign voices, he inhaled the unfamiliar aromas of food being sold from wooden carts. He noticed residential, commercial, and industrial sections as the trolley swayed, stopped, and started up again along the way. The clanging bell was loud and announced each upcoming stop.

As the streetcar approached center city, Sam observed men appearing in three-piece suits, looking like bankers or business owners. He was interested in the other riders but also drawn to the scenery outside as the route stretched more than twenty miles across the city. Sam had heard that it was the longest streetcar line in the United States.

After riding for about an hour, he arrived at the northern terminus where the route of the streetcar would reverse at a loop at Mermaid Lane. Sam exited the trolley and continued on foot, proceeding uphill on a street called Germantown Avenue. After several blocks, he saw a large three-story hotel with a covered porch, impressive residential dwellings, and numerous shops on the tree-lined street. People were strolling on the sidewalks. He was in Chestnut Hill. When Sam approached the busiest block of storefront businesses, he was fascinated and even more pleased when he saw a train station. Sam knew that convenience and transportation were important factors in deciding on a favorable place for his store. He became hopeful of someday owning a grocery market in Chestnut Hill.

My Grandfather's Grocery Store

My grandfather had a grocery store
on the busiest block in town.
The produce section resembled
an orchard in bloom
with apples, peaches, pears.
Vegetables gleamed with droplets of water.
Canned goods were piled high
like skyscrapers,
shelves filled with Corn Flakes,
salad dressing and spaghetti sauce.

The most popular spot was the meat counter
because my grandfather was a butcher.
He smiled to customers in a long white apron,
prided himself on offering
quality cuts of steaks and roasts
hanging there for all to view
or in parcels covered tight by plastic wrap.

Lined up in rows at the register,
I could reach with ease the candy display—
M&Ms, Milky Ways, and Tootsie Rolls.
My favorite memory was Martha,
the cashier who knew me well.
She let me choose one.

The store closed in 1955 and became
a fancy dress shop, a children's clothing store,
and later a toy store.
Today the floor area is divided
into sections where local artists sell
works of vibrant color.

Sentimental Reasons

My grandmother Pauline saved
my mother's report cards
in a folder from first grade
to college graduation

She smiled and held
my grandfather's arm
as their daughter
wearing a long white dress
reached for her diploma

My grandmother kept
love letters on scraps of paper
backs of envelopes
written by my grandfather
in artful penmanship

First light of morning
she would read his words
of love and appreciation
waiting for her by her place
at the breakfast table.

Chestnut Hill

On Germantown Avenue I'm a child
holding my grandmother's hand,
rewarded with the usual visit
to Frigate's bookstore
to graze among the shelves.

Smiles are like wildflowers
as we amble on the Avenue,
cobblestone streets echo
the faint clap of hooves
with the cadence of a past century,
steel tracks embedded as rails
for the 23 Trolley.

After passing stone homes with polished
front door knockers,
local eateries, tailor and greeting card shops,
we see our reflections in storefront windows,
Kilian's Hardware, Robertson's Florist,
and my grandfather's grocery store.

Before there were supermarkets
he offered fresh produce and choice cuts
of meat to choosy customers,
proud in his white butcher's apron,
until he retired to catch the morning train
and deal downtown at the stock exchange.

One time I tripped on the crooked sidewalk,
fell flat cutting my hand
when the Coke bottle I carried broke
and soda pooled on the pavement.
Blood dripped down my arm—
I looked away from the pain of six stitches.
The white line still visible decades later.

Yesterday My Grandfather Morris was Buried at the Cemetery

but I notice him
crouching behind the swings
at the playground
in a red Phillies hat he wore
at a game he went to last summer.

He hides in a pile of leaves
clinging to his sweater
blinks his brown eyes
as he squints
to keep out the dust.

Last week I sat on his lap
he spoke to me
retelling stories of his youth,
his skin sagged,
his voice hoarse.

His accent had a musical sound
I placed my finger in the cleft of his chin
his arms around me
cozy like sipping hot chocolate
after ice skating.

He watches me play
Looks after me still
I recall how
his crooked fingers
cupped my chin
telling me I was beautiful.

*(left) My grandparents
Pauline Goldberg and Samuel
Blumenthal as an engaged
couple, c 1920*

*Facing page: (upper)
My grandmother Rose
Silverquit Perch with her
Deitch cousins in Philadelphia
celebrating the ratification of
the 19th Amendment, 1920;
(lower) Wedding portraits of
Samuel Blumenthal
and Pauline Goldberg
Blumenthal, 1921 in
Philadelphia*

*Samuel Blumenthal and Pauline Goldberg Blumenthal standing
near their home in Chestnut Hill, Philadelphia, c 1934*

*(right) My grandmother
Rose Perch's cameo pin*

*(below) Newlywed portrait
of my grandparents Rose
Silverquit Perch and
Morris Perch, married
December 31, 1919*

BLUMENTHAL & HAYMAN
FANCY FRUIT AND PRODUCE
QUALITY GROCERS
PRIME SELECTED MEATS, FISH, POULTRY
BUTTER AND EGGS

8512-14 GERMANTOWN AVENUE

My grandfather Samuel Blumenthal and his delivery truck for Blumenthal & Hayman in Philadelphia, c 1930

MY FATHER

Discovering Those Precious Words

1

I discovered nine letters Dad had written
in 1944, addressed to his grandparents,
tucked away in an envelope,
boxed with old family photographs.
A 23-year-old soldier in basic training.
Sentences, phrases, thoughts,
perhaps describing his impressions
of an army base in Mississippi,
when all he ever knew
was city life in Philadelphia.

2

Feeling grateful
to come across an unexpected gift,
Dad's words, before he became Dad,
before he met my mother.
He was a grandson in 1944,
a great-grandfather in 2016,
when he passed away.
Generations bridge and blend,
shuffled like a deck of cards,
ever-evolving roles in a family.

3

What will these pages reveal?
What was on his mind and heart
during that uncertain time of war?
I'm anticipating, wondering,
but first they must be translated.
After all, the precious letters are in Yiddish,
the language of his grandparents.

When Memory Becomes Art

M Y AUNT was an artist. She painted still life using color, shade, and contrast. Sometimes a rolling landscape, impressionistic portraits of her children in watercolor, acrylic or oil. She attended art classes all her life and was hard on herself, never acknowledging her talent. She kept her collection, not selling paintings or even giving them away.

In her late 80s, she painted a vision from her childhood. It was a glimpse of a moment in time when her older brother played the tuba in the high school marching band. Although the hues were muted browns, grays, and greens, her brother holding his instrument of gold, dressed in a bright white uniform with red stripes, was the central focus.

Painted details revealed the form of a neighbor who lived in an adjoining apartment, inquiring if the family had pet seals. What were those strange sounds she had heard bellowing late at night through the common walls? A recollection, like a dream of so long ago, my aunt had expressed in shapes, words, and color on canvas.

She carried the painting to her brother at his assisted living residence. He had recently celebrated his 90th birthday. Brother and sister. A shared history of parents, childhood, and entangled bonds of a lifetime.

Holding her breath, she held up the painting to give him a closer view. She was blinking back tears of love and anticipation, hoping they would exchange knowing looks, smiles, and laughter, recalling a humorous event.

His face was without expression.

After the visit, my aunt tucked her memory back into the large plastic bag. Her footsteps on the linoleum floor echoed in the hallway as she returned from the building to her car and placed the package on the backseat. Later, my aunt will decide to wrap up the painting of that childhood experience in heavy brown paper and deliver it to the post office where it will be labeled fragile. The night before, she will write an explanation describing everything held in her heart about the incident, inspiring her artwork. I will receive a large package, an unexpected gift. I will be surprised and delighted to read how proud she was of her big brother in her heartwarming missive and discover a painting of my young Dad as a high school tuba player.

What My Father Always Said

Dad always said
Three kings and two queens, my full house
when he talked about us—his five kids.

Dad always said
This too shall pass
his way of providing comfort during difficult times.

Dad always said
When you get older things grow on you
I thought he meant skin tags and brown spots,
I now think he meant feelings and people.

Dad always said
I'm still here
his greeting when we visited him in assisted living.

And I will never forget he said,
Have someone to love,
Interests you love to pursue, and
Plans you love to look forward to.

I appreciate Dad's philosophy
as he aged he worried less—
took joy in family, books,
and being surrounded by his collections

My Father Collected Penguins

Because he was a collector
of all sorts of things
from art to zebras
at one time he fell in love
with penguins

He told us penguins fly
through the water not the sky
diving deep into the world
of dreams—huddled together
—no wonder he held us close
calling us his chicks

We searched for penguin gifts
on holidays and his birthday
mugs, pottery, framed artwork
sculpture, books, sweaters

until the day came when
he requested we stop
giving him penguins
we wondered why
but he laughed and said
his collection was complete

Although he asked us
to cease gifting them
I will always associate
flightless seabirds with him
displaying mine like lucky stars
because at one time
he fell in love with penguins

My Father Shines Like a Lighthouse

Following along hallways to his room
familiar with nursing home sights and smells
his door ajar, half asleep in his lounge chair

he's there, like a photograph
from his youth, the same expression
I move closer touching his hand and notice

flashes of dimples, a renaissance man,
collector of art, ephemera, and the extraordinary,
appreciation for objects with a curious story.

He speaks like he's in a dream filled with violin
music, always in love with the classics and piano
he wrote a song years ago recorded on vinyl.

I notice he's grown thin and wonder—
are they feeding him properly?
Have they forgotten to call him at mealtime?

A face transformed by hollow cheek bones
even at 95 that head of white hair—
now becoming thin and wispy.

"Where are your glasses?"
"They're lost or maybe I stepped on them."

I realize what I had taken for granted,
my lighthouse is crumbling, stumbling.

I feel an ache in a place he's grown too small to fill,
missing him even though he's still right there.

My Father's Voice

As I examine old photos
with a careful eye
and sort possessions
that may someday
be tossed away,

I bring attention
to important items,
so they shine like diamonds.
Everyone will know
what should be preserved

as my father did
when he placed
photos and documents
inside plastic sleeves,
arranged envelopes

with typed labels,
photos with dates,
handwritten notes
on the back.

Even though
he is gone
he calls out,
"Look at this, read this, keep this!"

When Memory Becomes Art *(2010) painting of my father
Gilbert Perch playing the tuba, by his sister Alma Perch Finestone*

(right) My father Gilbert Perch, c 1944

(below) My great-grand parents Louis Pecrch and Fannie Deitch Perch, c 1942

(left) My father Gilbert
Perch and his sister Alma
Perch, c 1932;

(below) One of the many
labeled pieces of memorabil-
ia collected by Gilbert Perch;
Two penguins from
Gilbert's collection

— BABA * MARRIAGE & DIVORCE —
PAPERS FROM SAM SILVERQUIT

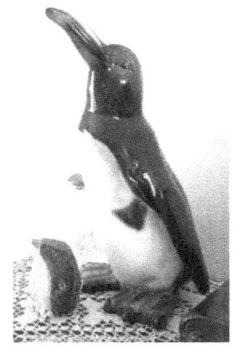

(left) Perch siblings:
(top row) Gary,
Andy, Brad,
(bottom row) Lois,
Judy, c 1980

MY MOTHER

My Mother Walked to
John Story Jenks School

I could be stepping in her footprints
as I navigate the crooked sidewalks
on the same route to school
my mother skipped along
in her charming hometown where
I have chosen to spend the weekend
celebrating my birthday.

I gaze into the August sky
at the building constructed in 1923,
the same year my mother was born,
this Late Gothic Revival,
three-story yellow brick facade,
with cement steps, stonewalls,
and unique architectural features
hidden by towering trees.

She would be delighted to find me here
admiring the nearby historic water tower.
My mother—running late even as a child,
dashing through the neighborhood,
carrying a book bag, a sweater,
curly hair tangled by the wind.
Her footprints can be found all over town.

My Mother was a City Girl

she grew up one block
from Germantown Avenue,
a bustling area with
banks, restaurants, shops,
her father's grocery store.

The cobblestone street
imbedded with steel tracks
the route of the 23 Trolley—
the longest line in the city,
weaving past row houses,
schools, car dealerships.

She grabbed the pole
stepped up on the 23,
dropped coins in the slot,
traveling east to shop in center city,
see a show, go to a museum,
breathe in the downtown air.

And mornings she could be seen
running down the sidewalk,
curls flowing,
swinging a bag of textbooks,
boarding the 23 Trolley
to take her west to college.

When My Mother Got Her Driver's License

WAVING GOODBYE as he backed down the driveway, Dad left for work steering his light green 1955 Olds sedan towards the city. He always wore a white shirt and a tie. Mom stayed home, seeing three of us off to school at the front door in her quilted pink bathrobe, checking school bags, handing out lunches while holding the baby over her shoulder. The bus stop was directly across the street, just steps from our door. Mom had our favorite chocolate chip cookies waiting when we hopped off the bus, aromas of dinner coming from the kitchen. Since she didn't drive, grocery shopping was scheduled with Dad on Saturdays.

I remember watching Mom get into a car with a strange man a couple of times. I had a knot in my throat wondering what was going on. Who was he? Where were they going? When we asked Dad, he didn't seem concerned but avoided giving an answer.

Surprise! We soon discovered he was a driving school instructor. Mom grinned, holding up her new driver's license and waving it like a flag. The second surprise was parked in front of our house, a blue and white 1959 Chevy Kingswood station wagon, a second car perfectly sized for our family. We piled in claiming our territory noticing that new car smell.

Summertime, Mom was behind the wheel wearing big sunglasses as we proceeded to the swimming club, the ribbon-cutting of the Cheltenham Shopping Center, and a family favorite, the Elkins Park Library. She was the mother of two young teens, a preteen and two toddlers. With her license and a car, Mom was liberated. She attended meetings of the PTA and League of Women Voters, as well as shuttling us to art and piano lessons, baseball practice, friend's houses, pediatrician and dental appointments. She even found time to be a Girl Scout leader and a den mother.

In ten years times changed. Dad transitioned to a new working arrangement. Mom got a job as a social worker. At first she drove the station wagon to work. Later she parked it at the local train station, a more convenient mode of transportation when her office was relocated to downtown Philadelphia. We all helped with dinner preparations by way of telephoned-in directions from Mom.

When Mom retired after 20 years with the Department of Social Services, she wasted no time lining up volunteer opportunities. One position was at Chestnut Hill Hospital working in the ER. She kept families informed of the condition and treatment of loved ones. The other was as a docent at a downtown Jewish museum. She loved the excitement of center city.

When Mom and Dad moved to a smaller place with no stairs, we helped them pack up and unpack. Their most cherished possessions, like the ornate music box, glass covered bookcases, and antique china cabinets filled with collectibles fit cozily into the new apartment. Familiar artwork covered the walls.

Gradually Mom developed glaucoma and macular degeneration. She had to give up driving and relied on Dad to take her where she wanted or needed to go. That wasn't her style, and the transition didn't come easily. For a while, a "companion" was hired to take Mom shopping and out to lunch, but that ended when it was discovered the companion was shopping with Mom's credit card.

She was not a complainer, but we noticed her voice became flat and there was a new edge to her personality. Looking back now I see more clearly the changes and disappointments she must have been going through. Her independence gone. Her adventurous spirit and activities restricted. Perhaps she was depressed about growing older.

Mom resided in a nursing home in her later years. She was in a wheelchair by then with low vision. At times in frustration, she would pepper the staff with caustic remarks. We would cringe when those exchanges happened during our visits.

"What is your education? Where did you go to school?" She made fun of their accents. "Don't you know how to pronounce my name? It's not Shoily, it's Shirley. Say it! Say it!"

Dad was located in the same continuing care complex in the assisted living section. When we visited, we got them together. Two people who had been married for 65 years were now separated by elevators, winding hallways, and an enclosed breezeway. Dad preferred we bring Mom to his room. That way, they were surrounded by their precious possessions.

In the company of her family her outlook mellowed, and she sometimes allowed us to push her along but Mom always knew exactly where she wanted to go.

My Mother Loved Dining *al fresco*

I recall those words
in her memory
when eating outdoors.

She planted annuals
in containers leading
to our front door
with colorful garden gloves
watering and pruning
red geraniums.

Summers she rested
in a lounge chair
by the pool at the swim club
beside a tower of magazines and newspapers
she hadn't found time to read
in a turquoise bathing suit
supervising our swimming.

Most of all she adored the beach
wearing a wide-brimmed hat,
settled in a beach chair
low to the sand,
beside a tower of magazines and newspapers,
slathered with sun screen,
sunglasses waving
as we bobbed in the ocean.

Rolling her wheelchair
to the garden of the nursing home
on a fall afternoon
a large tree provided shade,
I removed my sweater
hugging it around her shoulders.

Wearing My Mother's Jewelry

When I need to capture her spirit
I choose one of Mom's
rings or bracelets,
especially my favorites.
I remember her small hands, slim wrists,
straight fingers with slightly enlarged joints,
arms that hugged tight.

She wore a ring crafted
from a sterling silver spoon handle
wrapped around her finger.
I discovered it hidden
under a jumble of costume jewelry.
She bought it as I recall,
at an arts and crafts festival
in New England.

Now I share her taste
collecting beaded bracelets
and rings of twisted, braided silver,
mounted with gems of earth tones,
reminding me of her.

Best Mom

Standing in front of the kitchen cabinet
on the shelf with many mugs,
I pick the one that says
"Best Mom"—
the one with a colorful bloom.
It's not mine
but one I saved from Mom's house
when we cleaned things out.

A thick ceramic mug,
heavier than most,
sturdy I would say.
I place it on the Keurig
and aroma blossoms.
Coffee drips in a slow steady stream
with a whirling sound
while steam rises.

I sip warm feelings of her,
remembering what it was like
to have Mom
to talk with about anything.
Now I have to think
what to say and to whom.

Yahrzeit Illuminations

I gaze at the glow of my mother's yahrzeit candle,
burning near the bottom of the tall glass container
provided by the funeral home nine years ago,
based on the Jewish calendar,
lit last night at sundown, prayers recited.

Early morning house is silent,
except for the hum of the refrigerator.
The flame flickers, do I hear her voice?
I take my final sip of coffee,
washing down breakfast and memories.

Flashes of her life stored in albums,
boxes, envelopes, on my camera roll.
A child pushing a doll carriage,
at the beach with friends and family,
beloved daughter, beautiful and radiant,
college graduate between proud parents.

Golden years not easy,
mobility and low vision issues.
Although it was not unexpected,
we were dazed when she died suddenly
without a struggle, thank goodness.
A life well lived, she loved and was loved.

Getting Through Winter

Ordinarily an upbeat person,
my mother became depressed in winter.
A therapy light was recommended
to keep by her side for a period of time each day.
She looked forward to the Philadelphia Flower Show,
it meant spring was coming.

Because of the virus, we aren't snowbirds this year.
We were spoiled by the vibrancy
of tropical surroundings,
deep green palm trees,
against a cobalt sky.
Efforts to get through this unfamiliar winter
seem monotonous, like the repetitive routine of our days.
When sunlight pours into the kitchen,
we imagine it's warm outside.

I rescued certain plants before the frost
with the intention of nursing them through winter.
Watching over cuttings rooting in a glass,
transferred to potting soil,
to grow near windows.
From appearances,
it's uncertain if these plants
will thrive until spring.

In the winter of 2002, a gift from my mother,
a beautiful book, *In Bloom: The Floral Art of Sara Steele*,
a watercolor rainbow of rich, dense colors.
I came across it recently,
looking again, for the first time.
Remembering that Mom had always
provided messages.
Her inscription to me read,
Flowers are coming.

(left)My mother Shirley Blumenthal Perch in the garden with me at Stapeley at German-town in Philadelphia, 2011

(below) My mother Shirley Blumenthal, 1928

*(upper) Shirley's tea mug; Shirley Perch at Blue Bell Inn, 1990;
(lower) my parents Gilbert and Shirley Perch at the home in
Chestnut Hill, Philadelphia where Shirley grew up, c 1995*

(clockwise from upper left)Shirley Blumenthal and her cousin David Hecht at her home, c 1935;
Shirley Blumenthal's graduation from Chestnut Hill College 1944;
Shirley Blumenthal on Germantown Avenue in front of her father's grocery store, c 1940

MY FAMILY

7947 Heather Road

1950s—our stone and stucco,
chocolate brown, wood-trimmed,
semi-detached home,
a puzzle piece, part of an identical pattern
lined up and down the street.

Against the side of the house,
peony bushes with tight buds
attracted ants and bumblebees
feasting on sweet nectar,
pink blossoms popped each year.

Our grassy backyard
smelled of honeysuckles,
a swing-set and slide sat on gravel,
a stone wall to climb,
a walkable ledge from which to jump.
More fun than any store-bough toy.

A small patch of front lawn
with a mature oak tree.
Years later, that trunk remained scarred,
after Cindy, a neighbor girl,
a daredevil on her bike, popped the curb—slam!
Dad carried her home.

1112 Melrose Avenue

Lilting laughter in the center hall,
I looked over the railing,
framed by a sea of white spindles,
my toddler brother and sister twirled like tops,
their arms and eyes wide open,
heads back, giggling, probing possibilities
of this newfound space.

A summer day in 1961,
we moved into our new home.
Skipping up the walkway,
I kicked pebbles into the grass
delighted about the white frame house.
To view the height of three stories,
I leaned back, shaded my eyes from the sun
noticing floating cotton clouds.

The ceiling of the wraparound porch was pink
like the first geraniums of spring.
Front door ajar beckoned like a new friend,
revealing hidden stairways, dark closets,
stories of ghosts in the basement.
Like an explorer I ventured upstairs,
hand on the smooth wooden banister,
climbed to the second floor,
first sight of my new bedroom.

I remember the musty smell,
echoes in empty rooms.
Soon there would be painters, cleaners,
movers hauling in furniture,
screens placed in open windows
allowing the breeze to flutter drapes,
aromas of cookies baking,
filling up this home and our hearts with
a lifetime of delicious memories.

Ode to an Antique Music Box

When you were delivered to our home
we pored over every inch of you,
learning how you worked,
fascinated with a relic built in 1892.

With a special key Dad discovered
secret workings beneath your lid.
He pointed out the crank, switch, and fastener
releasing magical music.

Your fancy-footed, carved oak base
and matching music box sitting on top
were welcome additions
to a corner of the living room
across from the square grand piano.

When my youngest brother played you
for guests, he reached into your cabinet,
shuffling through a collection
of punched metal discs, choosing
Sousa marches to demonstrate your skills.

Musical notes reverberated with precision,
clear tones like bells and xylophones—
eyebrows raised, smiles on faces,
you were loved and adored.

We sailed off to follow our own music.
You aged at home with Mom and Dad,

developing nicks and scratches,
moving from place to smaller place
until it was just you and Dad in assisted living.

One of his favorite possessions,
you stood behind his lounge chair,
mostly silent, but at times you were
cranked up to play Sousa marches
as we reminisced about old times.

Dad grew thin — he fell, he wasn't well.
He moved to the safety of nursing care,
we gathered to empty his room.
Surely my youngest brother,
now a gray-haired man, would take you.

Truthfully, all of us wanted you
but when the time came
no one, not even my youngest brother,
was able to take you home.
What would become of you?

You were moved to the parlor,
a living room of sorts for residents and visitors,
your antique appearance a good fit
beside overstuffed sofas and chairs.
You entertained with Sousa marches
to the delight of those adoring smiles.

Summers

It was summer, ages six and five,
my brother and I
sharing a birthday party
in the backyard bedecked with streamers,
scents of cut grass, honeysuckle,
and sunbeams.
Donkey poster tied to the fence,
cake topped with frosted flowers,
pointed party hats, wrapped gifts,
rainbow of balloons.
We cruised around the driveway on
matching shiny red scooters.

Another summer, ages 10 and 9,
mounting our bikes
with neighborhood kids
perfecting skills with juicy pink bubblegum,
dreaming of adventures, maybe
to Wall Park, daring to place pennies
on train tracks, to be flattened,
skipping stones in a shallow stream
and floating homemade paper boats.

Carefree summer, ages 15 and 14,
sauntering along together
in the evening on the boardwalk
in Atlantic City.
Dazzling lights, salty smell of the air,
bleeps, blings, jingles of the arcade,
rolling ocean waves, rolling chairs.
We were young teenagers,
not wanting to be seen with parents.
Still a few inches shorter,
I'm thinking, *why can't he be taller
and look like a boyfriend.*

A Visit With My Brother

I want to kidnap
this moment in time
I hold in my hand
like a delicate bird
looking into your green eyes
the same eyes I have known forever
being 11 months younger
you have always
been part of my world.

Our mother went to the library
for advice on sibling rivalry
we fought fiercely as children
finally outgrowing
that behavior when you grew taller and
stronger than I.

I'm reminded
of our parents
protective umbrellas
until they passed,
generations merging
like the continuous flow of traffic
blending on a highway.

Side by side
in times of pain and loss
happiness and celebration
assuming our places in line,
as the oldest,
watching our children
mature into adults.

My Sister's Flair for Fashion

She with the blue eyes
had a flair for fashion,
an eye for style, color,
attention to detail.
When her foot could reach
the pedal on the floor,
Grandmother Rose taught her
to sew on an old Singer machine.

Home economics classes
in junior high,
she learned to work
with patterns, choose fabric,
pinning, cutting pieces
of her first clothing project,
a wrap-around red corduroy skirt.

She stitched an elegant A-line dress,
long and pink with a halter top
for me to wear to Singles Week
in the Catskills.
She was 12 years old.
I found a husband.

My Sister Continues to Shine

Using fabric of bold colors,
flowers, stripes, geometric designs,
durable texture,
her fingers edged the material
under the needle of the machine.

She designed, created, produced
yoga mat bags,
stitching love and pieces
of herself into fashioning
straps, pockets, and polka dot liners.

A time would come when
her star could no longer shine,
trying every treatment,
unable to continue.

All it takes to unravel
is to pull one harmless thread,
turns out it held everything
together. One person missing—
a link no longer in place.

After her bright light ceased,
an empty space remained.
Her signature bags
would become tangible,
radiant memories she left us.

How I Met My Second Husband

On an unmarked, unexplored path,
a detour, an escape route, a byway,
stinging from injuries and bruises,
no dreams or expectations,
still freshly alone, relieved,
mature but unaware,
unappreciated,
hiking along, eyes soft,
we collided at an intersection,
fell down together
and on best behavior
initiated conversation.

Two very different types,
we had lots to learn, to teach,
It made for careful listening,
patient explanations.
Moving slowly,
discovering common ground,
developing communication,
What makes you smile?
What makes me laugh?
Long bike rides, movies, books
for discussion.

In time, love arrived and settled in
like a carefree day at the beach,
Sand, seashells, wailing gulls
sailing just above the ocean currents.
Making plans to construct our lives
in a new formation,
Figuring it out together,
reinventing that unmarked,
unexplored path
where we started.

Closest to Your Heart

Not an unusual day at my desk,
Regular flow of work happening around me,
Co-workers, meetings, appointments.
A call from your doctor
cracked the mirror of my consciousness.
Words, words, and then I heard
"heart attack, meet him at the hospital"
You hadn't felt right for a few days.

At the hospital in minutes.
That's how it is in a small town.
I asked for you and was told
"Have a seat"
My face felt hot, my hands icy cold.
My name was called,
I followed to where you were lying
in an open room,
surrounded by medical scrubs.
One came forward and said
"He'll be taking a helicopter to DC"

Magically I found myself there,
sitting and waiting for direction,
for test results, for peace of mind.
Surgery was set to rescue your heart,
to reroute those arteries
not doing their jobs.

You woke up afterwards
with a nurse assigned to only you.
There was much to be thankful for.
Trying not to be overwhelmed by the tubes
and medical apparatus,
I focused on you,
your eyes half-closed,
your heart beating, pumping,
throbbing, thumping,
like it was brand new.

Family Treasures

The display in my dining room
is like a still life painting.
I hold a vase in my hands,
the painted one of blue glass with a red rose.
I feel the weight of family treasures
my daughters will not want.

What to do with delicate teacups,
matching saucers, gold rimmed glasses,
china with ornate design,
collections of figurines
my daughters will not want.

Many beautiful pieces collected
when we cleaned out the home
of my parents—framed art,
gravy boats, candlesticks,
a pedestal candy dish
once filled with nonpareils.

Objects belonging to my grandparents
with stories to tell if they could talk—
of fancy dinners, Seders, sitting
with friends for tea,
tarnished silver napkin rings
my daughters will not want.

(upper) Me and my sister Judy Perch Matour, 2016; and c 1968;

(lower) (standing) My brother Brad Perch and me; (seated) my brothers Gary and Andy Perch, at my birthday celebration at Blue Bell Inn, 2018

(upper) My sister Judy with our parents, c 1980
(lower) Perch Siblings: (l) Judy, Lois, Gary, Brad, Andy, 1998

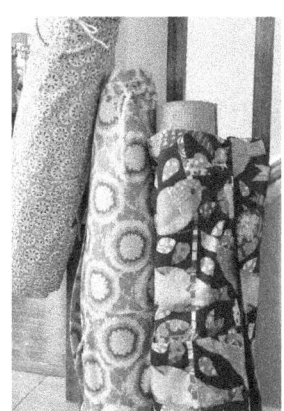

(upper) My husband Paul Villemaire and me at our wedding reception September 3, 1993; Yoga mat bags designed and created by Judy Perch Matour

(lower) My painting of our house on Melrose Avenue, Elkins Park, PA

(below) The house on Heather Road, Elkins Park, PA; (right) the author and her brother Brad Perch on the porch, c 1950

A backyard birthday party for Brad and me as we try out our new scooters, c 1954

The author and her husband Paul Villemaire at the Botanical Gardens in Naples, FL, 2023

The music box enjoyed for years at the Melrose Avenue home

ME

If You Ask Where I'm From, #2
after George Ella Lyon

I'm from day trips down the shore
to Atlantic City, sand, sunburn,
afternoons in the ocean with freedom
to ride the waves on a striped canvas raft.
Nights on the boardwalk, blinking lights,
rolling chairs, smells of popcorn,
sound of waves breaking on the beach,
collections of shells we brought home.

I'm from wading pools baking in the sun
in the backyard, filled by a garden hose.
I'm from digging to China, the smell
of summer, honeysuckle, and pine.
I'm from birthday parties, friends, balloons,
grandparents, pin-the-tail-on-the-donkey,
cakes with icing shaped like roses.

I'm from Girl Scout meetings,
selling thin mints door-to-door,
earning badges my mother struggled
to sew on my sash.
I'm from visits to the Franklin Institute,
moving through a two-story replica
of the human heart.
From aromas of my mother's brisket,
family dinners on Sunday nights
with my grandparents,
sitting on the floor watching Ed Sullivan.

I'm from collecting stamps like my father,
selecting from shelves of books at the library.
I'm from vegetarian vegetable soup,
looking for letters to spell my name.
Grilled cheese on Pepperidge Farm bread.
From riding my bicycle to piano lessons
with Miss Angel at her home on York Road.
I remember raking leaves in the fall.
Waiting for the magic of Polaroid photos to appear.

I remember the anticipation of starting school
and the excitement of the last day.
Running on the blacktop at recess.

I'm from soft pretzels sold on the street.
From Tasty-Kakes, Breyers Ice Cream
and corned beef sandwiches.
I'm from lighting Hanukkah candles,
tearing open gifts.
I'm from a family of tireless Phillies fans,
From going to my first major league game
with my father, astonished by the brilliance
of green grass and red seats.

I'm from special times with family.
Laughing, teasing, surprises, hugs—
enveloped by feelings of belonging.

Happy Birthday

On Heather Road
she squints into the sun
on her August 13th birthday,
the grassy backyard
smelling fresh cut
like a honeysuckle summer.

Showing off her white dressy dress,
an elastic string under her chin
holds a party hat on straight
atop a head of brown curls.

A ukulele swaying on a cord
across her shoulder,
she poses sweet as birthday cake
with a wide-eyed babydoll sitting
in her brand new stroller.

Kindergarten

I remember
my first day of kindergarten.
Mom gave me a kiss goodbye,
boys and girls squirmed on the carpet
listened to stories, took naps.

I picture
the old neighborhood,
hide and seek until lightening bugs
flashed in syncopated rhythm.
I fell asleep those summer nights
and dreamed of birthday parties.

I think back
to the awkwardness of turning twelve,
not anticipating body changes
—unwanted pounds.
Growing out of being a tomboy,
I still longed to feel the smack of the ball
connect with the swing of the bat.

I recall
my first time at a cemetery
when my grandfather died in '66
that sticky summer,
picked up at overnight camp,
taken home and protected within
the family cocoon.

I contemplate
the times I've heard my baby girls cry
learning sorrow can't always be consoled.
I juggled work and family,
released those tiny hands,
and sent them off to kindergarten.

The Scar

WHENEVER DAD TOLD THE STORY he would always say "the doctor sewed her up like a chicken." It happened the summer I was eight years old. We were playing in our suburban neighborhood like kids did in the 1950s, when the musical sounds of the approaching Good Humor man sent me dashing home for money for a popsicle. I loved the kind with vanilla ice cream covered by a coating of frozen milk chocolate, just like the giant one painted on the side of the truck.

As I shuffled between two parked cars to the sidewalk in front of our semi-detached home, I felt a scratch above my right knee and stopped to inspect. It didn't hurt but the sight of the deep red liquid beginning to stream down my leg like a small river was shocking. I found out later the culprit was a razor-sharp piece of metal sticking out from a damaged bumper.

I let out a scream! Someone raced into our house for help. Dad bolted down the four cement steps where I stood frozen on the sidewalk. By then I was sobbing due to the sight of my own blood.

"Get a diaper," he called to Mom who had stuck her head out the door. Having a new baby brother insured a supply of thick cloth diapers. She tossed one to Dad and he wrapped it tightly around my leg. Lowering my head towards the concealed laceration, I inhaled the pleasant aroma of laundry detergent and that special baby smell.

The next thing I knew he and I were in the '55 Olds heading to the pediatrician's office. It was just the two of us. Dr. Bittman ushered us to a treatment room and helped me onto an examination table covered with heavy white paper. Dad held me while the doctor removed the diaper. To make the experience even worse, he gave me a tetanus shot. I kept my head buried in Dad's chest as the doctor proceeded to stitch me up.

The thick pink scar has turned white over the years but remains—like an indelible memory.

From the Train

Dad dropped us off at the Elkins Park station
and waved goodbye from the window
of our 1955 green Oldsmobile 88.
We entered the stone building
with chocolate brown trim,
it smelled like cement floor and cigarette smoke,
benches lined the room, high ceilings echoed.

Mom led me by the hand to the counter,
opened her purse, pulled out her wallet
and bought to tickets to Reading Terminal.
Once downtown the tracks ended
so trains could reverse
and travel back to the suburbs.

We stepped onto the covered platform.
Our train would arrive from Jenkintown.
I looked down the tracks
careful to stay away from the edge.
My stomach lurched to imagine
what a scary fall that would be!
A bright beam signaled the approaching engine.

We found seats, I slid over to the window.
The clickety-clack lulled me,
the conductor punched our tickets.
Mom pulled a book from her schlep bag
as I leaned my head against the glass
and watched the world open up.

I Remember Bobby

I WAS IN THE 4TH GRADE in 1957. School, classmates, and family were my world. That year, I especially remember Miss Harvey and Bobby Carlin. Our teacher, Miss Harvey had shocking red hair. She was popular and everyone wished to be in her class. Each winter at the holiday assembly, Miss Harvey sang Oh Holy Night, harmonizing with the music teacher. On stage, they were a contrasting pair—one tall with red hair and the other, short with black hair. I looked forward to hearing their blending voices.

Miss Harvey created an opera club, inspiring a group of nine-year-olds to absorb her passion for opera. One masterpiece at a time, she explained the storyline and played the music until we knew it well. We learned terms like aria, libretto, and mezzo-soprano. The highlight was a trip downtown to a real production. We were thrilled to experience the characters of Carmen coming alive in costume and performing familiar songs with the rich sound of the orchestra.

My other 4th grade memory—Bobby Carlin threw in up class. He was a friendly boy, chubby with dark hair. Throwing up at school was awful but not unusual. The janitor rolled a bucket filled with soapy water and a wet mop into the classroom as we lined up for recess. Afterwards, we returned to the strong smell of cleaning products, the windows partly open. Bobby waited in the nurse's office for his mother to take him home. He remained absent all week and then all month.

They said he went into the hospital. In art class, we made get well cards and waited for news about when he would be coming back. His desk was unoccupied, the chair pushed in.

Bobby never returned to school. He had a brain tumor and passed away. Miss Harvey notified our parents so that the unimaginable news could be explained at home.

In the spring, his mother and father came to school for the planting of a tree next to the playground in Bobby's memory. I remember them standing silently together holding hands, heads bowed. How heartbroken they must have been, surrounded by a circle of children, none of them Bobby.

In the 1980s my Mom and I were at a social event and I saw her talking with a woman I didn't recognize. She motioned me over. "This is Mrs. Carlin, Bobby's mother."

"Oh hello, Mrs. Carlin, it's nice to see you again."

"Do you remember him? Bobby?" she asked.

I was surprised. "Of course, I do. We were in Miss Harvey's 4th grade class together."

Mrs. Carlin's voice softened. "It makes me happy to be with someone who remembers him. He had such a short life."

There was a bit more conversation that revolved around her son. I noticed her hopeful expression as she consumed the sweet memories with shining eyes and a melancholy smile. Miss Harvey had explained that many operas end tragically in death.

What I Remember is the Last Day of School

Miss Harvey's 4th grade classroom,
excitement beneath the surface,
like soapy bubbles blown through a wand.
She had all she could do to keep us settled down.

The room was electric and stuffy,
scents of summer flowers wafting
through half-opened windows,
shades half-closed to block the heat of the sun.

Yellow and black buses lined up
like bumblebees,
snaking around the parking lot,
Miss Harvey would release us before lunch.

Report cards distributed, blackboard erased,
desks emptied, papers stuffed into school bags,
search of the coat closet completed,
all belongings claimed.

The bell rang out for dismissal.
Wooden chairs scraped the green linoleum floor,
Miss Harvey's red head bobbing, nodding,
with wishes for a wonderful summer.

Outside on the blacktop
in our own frantic formation
freedom stretched out before us
like a batch of birds against the sky.

The Ball Collector

WE FOUND OUT about her death because Dad saw her obituary in the newspaper. A week or two later, her property was posted with a sign advertising the sale of the contents of her home. Dad collected antiques and anything old. He was anticipating treasures waiting inside to be discovered. I gripped his hand as we walked down the path and up the steps to the large front porch of the house next door. I wanted to enter but felt like we were trespassing - invading her privacy. Being inside her house was like an unsolved mystery.

"Is it okay for us to be here?"

"Yes, it's fine. Don't worry, honey."

For two years I thought we lived next door to a witch. She was an old lady, alone in a large, three-story house made of stone. We didn't know much about her but neighbors said that she was a retired high school math teacher and had never married. At one time, she had lived in this house with her parents and an older brother, but they died long ago.

She was skinny and wore knitted shawls over long, flowered dresses. As her head shook slowly from side to side, she walked awkwardly with a cane and her white hair was pinned up. Her face was mapped with wrinkles, and she wore wire-rimmed glasses . We were warned by the other kids that if a ball should accidentally land her yard, it was lost forever. When my brother once tried to sneak over the hedge to retrieve a football, she appeared and yelled out in a shrill, shaky voice "Get off my property," waving her cane in the air.

I was eleven years old when we moved into the neighborhood. My bedroom window on the second floor faced the side of her house. A few feet of lawn and the width of her driveway separated us. At times I saw her moving around in her kitchen or washing dishes at the sink in front of the window. Once she looked up and saw me. I was ashamed of myself for spying.

Every week she entered the garage to start up her old black Ford. She would back it halfway down the driveway where the engine would run for about fifteen minutes. Then she returned it to the garage. Sometimes I watched this ritual from my window. I never saw her drive the car on the street.

The house was packed with noisy, curious people handling and inspecting her furniture, clothes, and framed art. The air smelled like old books. Dust was floating in the bright sunbeams shooting between the open blinds. There were old steamer trunks filled with fur coats, hats, shoes, and purses. There were no toys.

"How much for the piano?" Dad asked the man greeting customers and collecting money.

He purchased the square grand that would be moved to our living room. He also bought an antique music box and two old trunks.

"Dad, what's in the trunks?" "That's the fun of it. We'll find out when you unpack them at home."

When I was brave enough to leave his side, I wandered around afraid to touch anything. Family photos stared from the walls. I covered my eyes and imagined that she, along with her parents and brother were watching me. I tripped over a box and threw out my hands to break my fall. I clapped them together to clear off the dust from the floor.

There were piles of folded linens, stacks of china, and tarnished silverware. I found myself in the kitchen and from the window, it was strange to see our house. I contemplated her view of our busy family while she was there alone. Living with my Mom, Dad, three brothers and a sister, I could never imagine being alone. My two sets of grandparents visited often, and I sometimes stayed overnight with them playing cards, celebrating holidays, looking at old family photos and telling stories. There was always candy or an ice cream cone.

Her possessions were on display like in a museum or a garage sale. There had been no grandchildren in her life. I felt a throb of loneliness in this gray house that was gradually being emptied by strangers.

I needed to find Dad and ask if he were ready to leave. Backing out of the room, I spotted an old wicker laundry basket sitting in the corner filled to the top with balls. Mystery solved—she was finally giving them back.

On Not Choosing Paper Dolls

You sat at your skirted dressing table
searching for happiness in the mirror,

understanding little league for you
was a dream that could never come true.

You challenged the boys on the field,
your brothers and others on the block

playing baseball on summer days. In the fall
you asked your mother to cancel ballet

she finally relented and agreed you could play
Saturdays on the neighborhood team.

"Girls pick up jacks or dress paper dolls."
You did—but it wasn't your first choice.

With chalk you drew hopscotch on the sidewalk,
hop hop hopping on one foot wasn't the same.

You watched your brothers and friends
from your seat in the stands at the little league game,

born too soon to be included,
to venture where girls were not accepted.

I think of that tomboy whose youthful mind
never imagined barriers tumbling with Title ix.

Turning Myself Over To the Sea

Floating on my back
the current becomes a compass

and guides my course,
my mind is calmed as the water

surrounds and holds me,
Wrapped in the arms of the sea,

feeling safe settles the surging
of my restless thoughts.

I pause in the wavy blues and greens
squinting into the sunlight above.

Driving Lesson

WHEN I ASKED MY PARENTS for the car to go to the library with Lisa, I was sixteen years old and had been driving for only a few months. They had no reason to doubt me. I was never in trouble, no skipping school, bad report cards, or rebellious tendencies. But Lisa and I had a secret plan to surprise her boyfriend Ronny at his home in another part of the city. It was to be a quick visit—a chance for them to see each other. We estimated it would take 20 minutes to get to Ronny's and calculated that the visit and return trip would fit neatly inside the time frame of completing our homework assignment at the library, the cleverly concocted story. I confidently set off after dinner to pick her up in our 1963 Oldsmobile sedan.

We each assumed the other knew the route but soon realized that we both had no idea how to get there as we navigated beyond our neighborhood roads. Driving up and down Roosevelt Boulevard in northeast Philadelphia, we knew we were lost. Traffic was picking up on the busy boulevard. I was feeling anxious and my mouth was dry. We tried another direction, looking for landmarks or road signs that we recognized, but the streets all looked alike, lined with endless chains of row houses. Turning off the radio to concentrate, we realized the plan wasn't going well.

It was 1964. There were no cell phones or GPS. We didn't consider stopping at a telephone booth to call for help. Lisa was fifteen-years-old and not driving yet, so I was forced to continue. Discovering a street with a familiar name, we became hopeful, and I took a quick right turn. Following closely behind us was a car with its headlights shining like a beacon in my eyes through the rear-view mirror. Lisa turned around.

"It's a police car," she said.

I steered into the parking lot of a gas station. My heart was pounding in my ears, and I imagined that Lisa could hear it. I felt heat rising up my neck into my flaming face. The policeman approached my side of the car as I lowered the window.

"Young lady, you don't have your headlights on."

"Oh, I'm sorry."

The experience had become so nerve-racking that we hadn't noticed that it was getting dark. I pulled out the knob on the dashboard that controlled the headlights, and two beams of brightness flooded the area in front of the car.

"Driver's license and vehicle registration."

With shaking hands, I opened my wallet. Luckily, I knew that the registration was kept in the glove compartment. The policeman told us to wait and returned to his vehicle.

"Lisa, let's tell him the truth. I'm scared and tired of driving." I looked at my watch. It had been over two hours since I left home. My parents would be worried. When the policeman returned, we told him.

"There's a phone booth on the other side of the gas station. Call your parents. I'll wait nearby until they come."

In a booth that smelled like gasoline, we called home. I choked up while confessing the truth to my Mom. Before long, our dads pulled up in Lisa's family car. As she left the car, I moved over, and my Dad took the driver's seat. We proceeded home with little conversation.

At the front door, my Mom was waiting to pounce like a panther. I could see in her narrowing eyes that she was furious. Like the policeman, she asked for my license. I handed it to her, and she tore it to pieces. In 1964, a license was made out of paper. I felt relieved and didn't much care about the loss of that privilege. Driving had lost its appeal. I was happy to be safely at home even though I was in big trouble.

"You lied to us. We're taking away your telephone and you're grounded for three weeks. Go to your room." She turned her head toward the stairs and pointed as if to show me the way. Okay, I could live with that. But the unspoken lesson was worse. I had lost their trust in me.

Bottom of My Heart

The bottom of my heart is crowded.
It's where condolences wait to be shared.
Where love for my family resides.
Where I feel emptiness for special ones lost,
who will never be forgotten
or replaced.
Where there are empty spaces
that ache
Where regrets weigh heavy
even though I forgive myself.
Where optimistic faith nests
when the world is in turmoil.
Continuing to believe
words I heard as a child,
"Everything will be all right."
Where memories glow,
Preserving my parents
forever, reflecting the best of times.
Where feelings are buried,
bubbling up when least expected.
Where I find the inspiration to write,
excavating to the very bottom,
searching the deepest cavern,
making certain it can expand.

(left) With my father Gilbert Perch on the beach in Atlantic City, c 1955

(right) With my daughters Nikki Cooke (l) and Lori Finkelstein, c 1981

Shirley and Gilbert
Perch, c 1951

Family celebrating the Bar Mitzvah of my brother Gary Perch
(far right), c 1964

(left) Author's backyard birthday party on Heather Road, c 1951; (above) Author, c 1958

The author, her siblings and their families at a celebration in Philadelphia, 2013

Gratitude

I decided to direct my energies into writing after retirement in 2010. In a series of writing classes with Caroline Bock, I was introduced to a basic understanding of the craft. I soon discovered a wonderful conference held annually at St. John's College in Annapolis, organized by Lynn Schwartz and Laura Oliver. In this dynamic one-day seminar, consisting of author-speakers, compelling workshops, and meaningful connections, I met my dear friend, Barbara Schilling Hurwitz. We decided to meet or talk each month for accountability and to encourage and inspire each other in our writing efforts. That practice has continued and intensified from 2017 to this day. I thank her so much for urging me to move forward with this manuscript.

I thank Shuly Cawood for her helpful classes, including "Let's Write Together." This prompt-writing workshop has fueled my imagination and inspired ideas for many of my poems.

My thanks to Laurel Benjamin and Lorette C. Luzajic. Laurel has organized and led a series of very successful virtual Ekphrastic workshops. Lorette is the editor of *The Ekphrastic Review,* as well as an accomplished artist, writer, and instructor.

I first became acquainted with Jodi Paloni when she read a

portion of one of her short stories at an on-line *Press 53* session. I was inspired to purchase and read her book, *They Could Live With Themselves.* Jodi has helped me assemble this book and I'm grateful for her wise suggestions, organizational expertise, and coaching skills.

A special thanks to my cousin Cheryl Blumenthal for her continued support.

To my husband Paul, my heart appreciates your kindness, patience, and positivity, topped with an abundance of caring and sharing. Your support and love make life easier to navigate.

Finally, to my entire family: I want you to know how important you are to me.

Biography

Lois Perch Villemaire spent her childhood in a suburb of Philadelphia and moved to Annapolis, Maryland, in 1972. After working for the local library system, she enjoyed a career in county government. During retirement, she exchanged technical writing for creative writing and found inspiration in poetry and memoir flash. Her activities in family connections and research merged with writing and the idea for *My Eight Greats*, a family history in poetry and prose was conceived. Her work has appeared in literary journals such as *The Ekphrastic Review, ONE ART, Blue Mountain Review* and anthologies including *I Am My Father's Daughter*. Lois volunteers at the library, enjoys fun photography, yoga, and dotes over her growing collection of African violets.